THE POWER OF EXTREME WRITING

How do I help my students become eager and fluent writers?

Diana
CRUCHLEY

ASCD   Alexandria, VA USA

Website: www.ascd.org
E-mail: books@ascd.org

www.ascdarias.org

PAPERBACK ISBN: 978-1-4166-2084-6   ASCD product #SF115065

Also available as an e-book (see Books in Print for the ISBNs).

ASCD Member Book No. FY15-8B (July 2015 PSI+). Member books mail to Premium (P), Select (S), and Institutional Plus (I+) members on this schedule: Jan, PSI+; Feb, P; Apr, PSI+; May, P; Jul, PSI+; Aug, P; Sep, PSI+; Nov, PSI+; Dec, P. For details, see www.ascd.org/membership and www.ascd.org/memberbooks.

Library of Congress Cataloging-in-Publication Data
Cruchley, Diana, 1945-
  The power of extreme writing : how do I help my students become eager and fluent writers? / by Diana Cruchley.
     pages cm -- (ASCD Arias)
  Includes bibliographical references.
  ISBN 978-1-4166-2084-6 (pbk. : alk. paper) 1. English language--Composition and exercises--Study and teaching (Elementary) 2. Effective teaching. I. Title.
  LB1576.C8418 2015
  372.62'3--dc23
                              2015013059

21 20 19 18 17 16 15   1 2 3 4 5 6 7 8 9 10

THE POWER OF EXTREME WRITING

How do I help my students become eager and fluent writers?

ASCD MEMBER BOOK

Many ASCD members received this book as a
member benefit upon its initial release.

Learn more at: **www.ascd.org/memberbooks**

Want to earn a free ASCD Arias e-book?
Your opinion counts! Please take 2–3 minutes to give
us your feedback on this publication. All survey
respondents will be entered into a drawing to
win an ASCD Arias e-book.

Please visit
www.ascd.org/ariasfeedback

Thank you!

What is Extreme Writing?

Why do we need an all-new look at journaling and writing? I became aware of how much schools were neglecting the element of fluency, and I wanted to create consistent, long-term excitement about writing that would help students build that fluency. Extreme Writing is an intermittent, 20-minutes a day, 10-days in a row act of writing that students actually look forward to and want more of. It's fun, it's fast, and it works. How many times do your students actually ask for more writing? Extreme Writing is the first step in the right direction to making that happen.

Why is Extreme Writing important?

With regard to the anchor ELA standards and their emphasis on writing proficiency, the Common Core State Standards (CCSS) document states, "To meet these goals, students must devote significant time and effort to writing, producing numerous pieces over short and extended time frames throughout the year" (CCSSI, 2010). However, many teachers have difficulty getting their students to write anything at all, especially if students know their efforts will be graded. They may procrastinate, write skimpy drafts, write the minimum required, or even not write at all. Extreme Writing gives you a way to cultivate a writing culture that requires minimal classroom time and builds both fluency and enthusiasm for a skill that is critical to academic success.

You can only improve at something if you practice it often. Many athletes remark that they receive accolades for their great reflexes, top speed, and good understanding of game flow. What they don't mention is all of the practice, practice, practice that's required to be great. The research behind Malcolm Gladwell's book *Outliers* (2011) also stresses that intelligence and ambition are not enough—10,000 hours of work and practice are what produce results in the form of mastery. Unfortunately, we can't grant our students those 10,000 hours of exposure in the classroom, but we can come close and mimic the results with Extreme Writing.

The three skills students must have to be successful writers are code, comprehensibility, and fluency.

- **Code** refers to an understanding of the code of English, including elements such as reading left to right and top to bottom, along with spaces between words, punctuation, spelling, capitalization, and paragraph formation. All of these together convey the specific code used to represent English.
- **Comprehensibility** is the ability to write comprehensibly, which includes being able to write with clarity (so a reader can understand) and in the conventional forms of English (e.g., comparison, argument, description, essay, recipe, newspaper report, review)

- **Fluency** is the ability to perform the act of writing quickly. This is the neglected aspect of writing that Extreme Writing can help address.

When students arrive in high school, they may be facing eight subjects, each with its own homework assignments and daunting list of vocabulary to master. For example, in a high school biology text, there can be dozens of potentially unfamilar words, such as *organelles*, *plantae*, *autotropic*, *eukaryotic*, *chloroplast*, and *mitochondria*. It has been said that high school is a giant vocabulary lesson consisting of the words for multiple disciplines. Classroom and homework assignments must be completed quickly for each discipline.

Picture two students; let's call them Sylvia and Jon. Imagine they are equally clever and equally good at the code of English. Now imagine that they are able to write with equal levels of comprehensibility . . . but Sylvia has twice the fluency of Jon. This means that Sylvia's two hours of homework would take Jon four hours, which is a recipe for a lower grade not because Jon is less smart, able, careful, or hard working but simply because he is slower, less fluent, and therefore less productive.

Indeed, choosing a boy (Jon) and a girl (Sylvia) is more than an example. The 2007 National Writing Assesment used a 100-point scale. Girls in 12th grade averaged scores that were 20 points higher than boys. If a typical boy had 60 points, then a typical girl would have 80 (Salahu-Din, 2008).

Why is it called Extreme Writing and how does it work?

When coming up with a name for this process, I tried to choose a name that would express exactly as possible what it is—writing quickly, with few rules (other than neatness, fair spelling, and comprehensibility). It is much more than journaling. And besides, think about it, what sounds like more fun: "Take out your journals" or "Time for Extreme Writing"?

It's important to note that Extreme Writing does not replace full-scale writing process lessons. Instead, picture it as a side endeavor that focuses on fluency—the neglected third leg of the writing process.

None of the traditional five steps of the writing process (prewriting, drafting, revising, editing/proofreading, and publishing) explicitly teaches students to be fluent—to write quickly on a topic. Fluency is often thought of as an indirect product of all of the work students do in school, but we rarely engage with students to teach the skill directly. Extreme Writing offers a direct effort to produce fluent writers, and the spin-off to the traditional writing process becomes more exciting when students have self-confidence and are able to engage with it more quickly.

With this in mind, Extreme Writing assignments can take any form you (or your students) wish. Although you want students to write comprehensibly—in complete sentences with proper spelling—you should not focus on the details of grammar or structure during these assignments. Make sure students understand from the start that this is not a diary. Everything they write might be shared with the class, so they should not include anything they would not want everyone to know.

Introduce an enticing topic (I refer to them as Inspirations) and provide three prompts or possible topics the Inspiration might inspire. Students then spend about five minutes responding to any prompt they choose in class before taking it home and spending an additional 15 minutes there to finish the assignment. You don't *have* to make it a homework completion, but with a very demanding curriculum to cover in class, you may wish to.

How much should I ask my students to write?

I know what you're thinking. "If I ask my students to write for just five minutes in class and then 15 minutes at home, what's to stop them from writing three sentences and claiming that it took them the entire 15 minutes?" Well, to be honest, nothing. So how do you stop that? Ask for a specific number of words that they should be able to write in 20 minutes. This word count should be differentiated based on your assessment of individual students.

To that end, I suggest using the Rapid Write approach. In a Rapid Write, students begin with a blank page and the following instructions (or a variation thereof): "When I say go, you are going to have one minute to write anything you want. Start with what is on your mind at the time. You don't have to stay on a single topic, and it doesn't have to be organized, but it does have to be neat, spelled as well as possible, and readable by another student. Here's the catch, though:

you are not allowed to lift your pen or pencil to think. You have to keep writing. If you can't think of anything, it's okay to write 'I can't think of anything. My mind is blank. Maybe everyone else has a blank mind too and they are just writing. I can hear everyone else writing, but I have nothing to say.' Just keep going until you have something to write about or until the minute is up. Everybody ready, set, go!"

When time is up, ask students to count how many words they wrote and then write that number in brackets at the end of the text. Then have students start again for another minute on another piece of paper and try to "beat" their score. After a while, students will even "assume the racing position" by leaning forward with pens poised, waiting for you to say go. When this happens, you know they're engaged.

Students may also eventually ask to "do that Rapid Write thing again." This might be the first time they ask for Extreme Writing, but it won't be the last.

Collect students' pages and arrange them from lowest to highest word count. What is the student "in the middle" able to accomplish? (You should find that most students' word counts cluster around the median, or that middle student.) Once you have tallied the "scores" (i.e., the word counts), you may reveal to students what the middle value was—not the bottom and never the top. Current research on gaming theory says that a "leader board" is only motivating for those within striking distance of the leader.

If you take that middle number and multiply it by 20, you will get a good approximation of the maximum number of words students can write in 20 minutes. At this point, you might be saying, "But I told them not to think. And in Extreme Writing I want them to think." That's true. Imagine you have established that your students can write 300 words in 20 minutes. Subtract 50 for "think time" and maybe another 25 to give a little leeway (e.g., in case their hand gets sore). Then think of individual students' abilities. Because your least motivated students must remain in the game, you might subtract another 25 words to "level the playing field." In the end, you're left with a total of 200 words students must write in 20 minutes. Every student (except identified special needs students) gets the same goal number. For some, this is a challenge; for others, it's really easy. Just stay focused on the goal—it's about increasing fluency. This is where professional judgment plays a major role.

As students get faster and more fluent, they will increase their word count ability and be able to finish those 200 words in 15 or maybe even 10 minutes. Around the middle of the school year, conduct another Rapid Write and reassess the word count you can ask for and expect from your students. Use the same method of calculation, and you should find that the median (i.e., that middle student) is significantly higher. This is a great way to assess whether your fluency project is working.

Once you have recalculated a word count target (perhaps after the winter break), you could tell your students, "I am so proud of you. You're getting to be amazingly fast at writing your ideas and thoughts down. Being fluent writers is very good news for all of us. You can now write 200 words in a lot less than 20 minutes. Our class goal remains the same:

amazing fluency in 20 minutes. Therefore, I'm going to raise your number to 250."

Your students might complain, but, secretly, they will be proud of themselves. I have actually overheard students in the hallway say, "We can write so fast that our teacher had to assign us to write more!"

What Does Extreme Writing Look Like In the Classroom?

I don't intend Extreme Writing to be used every day, all year long. That would be boring, and our goal here is to be the *opposite* of boring. Instead, you do it every day for exactly two weeks—10 school days. Then you wait until the next month and do it for another 10 consecutive days. Repeat every month, and you end up with 8–10 sessions of Extreme Writing in a year.

Part of what makes Extreme Writing work is that it's incorporated into the curriculum in a way that keeps the process fresh, novel, and almost unexpected. Nevertheless, it should still be somewhat predictable in the amount of work required.

Let's think again of Malcolm Gladwell's *Outliers* (2011) and his concept that developing genius at anything takes 10,000 hours. If students write 20 minutes a day for 10 days in a row, at least eight times a year from 4th through 9th grade, then they will write an additional 9,600 minutes (i.e., 160 hours). It may not be 10,000 hours, but it is a vast improvement over basic writing process lessons and cross-curriculum writing mandated by the Common Core State Standards.

How do I plan my year?

Print a calendar of your school year. Block out the two-week segments you plan to use Extreme Writing. Select the types of Inspirations you will use (possibly from the list of 13 I've included in this book). Remember, though, that if you plan to use Extreme Writing throughout the year, you will need 100 Inspirations. It's important to have as much variety as possible, thereby keeping Extreme Writing as unpredictable as possible. Stay alert to student suggestions and interests as you go; remember that your secret goal is for them to beg for Extreme Writing.

Although students—indeed, all humans—want a predictable environment in order to successfully navigate their world, our attention is typically grabbed and engaged by something that is suddenly different. Why does interest in journaling decline through the years? In short, its repetitiveness and predictability is what eventually makes students sigh and roll their eyes when you ask them to take out a journal.

So how do we keep Extreme Writing from suffering the same fate? We make it relentlessly unpredictable.

- First, students do not know precisely when you are going to do it again. You know that Extreme Writing cycles consist of 10 two-week segments, but they don't.

- Second, an Extreme Writing book is very short. It's only 10 pages long, and then it is finished. There is nothing quite like the feeling of closing a book and knowing the "job is done."
- Third, the Inspirations have enormous variety from day to day.

What is an Extreme Writing book?

Use short notebooks—which can be filled up in two weeks—as Extreme Writing books for students. You could construct them yourself by stapling 10 pages onto a cardstock cover front and back. If possible, include an engaging design on the cover, such as a photo or drawing of someone skiing off a mountain, flipping on a skateboard, surfing a giant wave, or skydiving, along with the words *Extreme Writing.* Try to have a different book (and design) for each two-week period.

Students will write one page every day for 10 days, and then the book is "full." Almost all of the other books students use continue all year, and if they run out of pages, we simply add more. It's great to have something with an end so students can think, "I finished something, and it looks pretty impressive." It's an invaluable sense of accomplishment.

At the end of each 10-day session, collect the Extreme Writing books, and put each in a large manila envelope with the student's name on it. Keep them all in a banker's box, which should be stored prominently somewhere in the classroom. If you want, you can even decorate the box with wrapping paper, words, and pictures. Making it visible in this way makes it more likely that students will recall Extreme Writing and ask when they can do it again. You're going to do it anyway, but it is so very rewarding to have students ask for this productive work.

Save the Extreme Writing books for the entire year in that box. Having a set of eight Extreme Writing books at the end of the year really lets students recognize and reflect on their growth. Impress on your students that they should save a few examples of their writing. Point out that they may be famous someday and these will be worth a lot of money!

What's inside the book is even more important than what the outside looks like. Therefore, keeping a consistent format is important to finding anything in it afterward.

- Number the pages. This provides a sense of accomplishment.
- Remind students to include the full date, including the year and day of the week, whenever they write. (Optional: Include the starting and ending times.)
- Have students write or paste in each day's prompt before they begin their own writing.
- Where possible, provide a small, relevant visual that students can paste into their Extreme Writing books. This helps to make their entries more vivid.
- Tell students to draw a line under the entry when they're done writing. This provides an obvious visual clue for where they should begin next time.

What should students write about?

An Inspiration is something you present to capture attention and get students thinking. An example might be a photo of a shark attacking a man dangling from a helicopter. The three prompts are topics that call up a memory from students and asks for writing that is within their existing writing repertoire (i.e., a story). The following ideas are three potential prompts for the shark attack example:

- Tell the story of what is happening in the photo, what happened before this, and what will happen next.
- Tell about a time you "could have been killed."
- Tell any water stories you have experienced, such as learning to waterski, learning to swim, or playing in a waterfall or creek.

It is important to provide these prompts because it gives students a choice, which makes it harder for them to say, "I can't think of anything to write." It also provides an element of autonomy and allows students to decide for themselves what they want to write about.

Why three prompts? Having more than three choices can often immobilize a student's decision-making process, and totally free choice can result in students flailing about trying to think of something to write. Three choices isn't overwhelming, and it is a way for them to achieve the required number of words. If they run out of something to say with the first prompt, they can simply choose another one and continue writing.

To come up with appropriate prompts, think about the Inspiration you're using and consider what your students will likely have experienced or can imagine. Sometimes it is useful to have them write "everything they know about . . ."

Of course, there are thousands of prompts available online, but I've found that it is far better to start with an amazing Inspiration and then think of compelling prompts than it is to search for prompts and then imagine a suitable Inspiration. You want to engage students before they start to write. You want something novel to kickstart their minds. That is what an Inspiration does.

How Do I Assess Extreme Writing?

Look, I know you're already swamped. You don't need to mark every word your students write in their Extreme Writing books, but you can easily obtain a mark every day. Homework and classwork is most meaningful when it is responded to immediately (Dean, Hubbell, Pitler, & Stone, 2012). With this in mind, ask students to pass their papers to a partner or neighbor, and have students then count the number of words. (Imagine that you have established 200 words to be an appropriate target.) Make sure students are aware of and familiar with the following marking criteria:

5: You exceeded the request and wrote more than 220 words. (110%)

4: You wrote 190–219 words. (100%)

3: You wrote 150–190 words. (75%)

2: You wrote 100–149 words (50%)

1: You wrote 75–99 words (25%)

0: You wrote fewer than 75 words.

In this way, you can collect up to 10 marks a month. Extreme Writing assignments can't be assessed like you do for "normal" writing assignments since you didn't specifically teach anything. What you are assessing here are students who think and write faster. Why? Because fluency matters (and so does ideation—the ability to create a range of ideas).

Do I need to respond to student writing?

In a word, no. If you tried to respond to every student every day, you would exhaust yourself and give up on the process. On the other hand, homework is most effective when it is valued in the classroom afterward.

Peer feedback can be just as effective as teacher feedback, and it is often more motivating than your comments. I like to call the process a bivouac. Explain to students that a bivouac is an improvised campsite often made from whatever is available and used by hikers, mountaineers, and soldiers when they can't get back to base camp. It is a simple gathering place for two people. In class, two students should "form a bivouac"—they huddle together as a pair, read each other's entries, and provide meaningful comments. Remind students of how to provide respectful feedback and constructive criticism. Post the following sentence starters on the board:

- I didn't know that...
- I liked the part where you...
- I'd like to know more about...
- I didn't understand that part. Tell me more about it.

If you don't have time to bivouac every day, you could, for example, designate each Friday as a day for students to share the "best stuff" from their Extreme Writing. Allow five minutes for each student to review what he or she has written and highlight the best stuff. Then allow 10–15 minutes for small groups of four students to share with one another.

Bivouac (peer feedback) time is valuable because it provides an incentive for students to write. They'll want to have something to share with their classmates. Students not only share one another's experiences but also deepen their relationships. In addition, doing it once a week retains that element of unpredictability and fun we want. Just picture your students asking, "Are we going to bivouac about this?"

At this point, you may be saying, "I want to know what my students are thinking. I like them to know I care. I want to see how they are doing." Try this. Choose one or two Extreme Writing cycles and, using your class list, respond to a third of the class each day—just the content and thoughts, as you would with a journal. It's a great way to learn more about your students' thinking, but, if you feel you have to do it too often, or if you think you need to do it at all, it will become overwhelming. The danger there is that you will stop Extreme Writing and lose what it will accomplish for your students. Keep an eye on the big goal: fluency.

What Inspirations Can I Use?

Practice is essential to mastery, and repeated practice is critical. So, with the variety of Inspirations that follow, be prepared to repeat each type of inspiration at least three times over the course of a school year. Plan it out. That is, imagine one type of Inspiration you will use is a really exciting projected photograph. If you used one in September, and different ones in November, January, March, and May, it would still keep Extreme Writing fresh. It's not always a photograph, as that might take away the novelty, but photographs do recur during the year. By the way, giving students a miniature version of an Inspiration with the three prompts is a good idea. They can paste it into their journals to remind themselves of what they are writing.

Inspiration #1: Start with a Picture

The Internet is full of wonderful images. Students tend to gravitate toward three different kinds of pictures: "things that can kill you," "funny things," and "things that are unusual." To get you started, I've set up a Pinterest page with several dozen images and prompts (www.pinterest.com/diana32/extreme-writing-journaling-photos).

For example, imagine a picture of a proud-looking bird with a mouth full of little twigs ready for a nest. The prompts could be

- Tell about a time you built a fort (inside or outside, summer or winter).
- Discuss everything you know about birds.
- Tell a story about building with blocks and toys (LEGO, Minecraft, etc.) or about something you have built.

Remember that you really only need 10 images in order to use this Inspiration for a whole year, unless your students start asking for it more often—at which point you are mentally saying, "gotcha!"

Inspiration #2: The Extreme Jar

Each student should have his or her own jar, about the size of a baby food jar, filled with 30 writing prompts. At the beginning of the year, you can have students cut up a sheet of prompts into strips and put them in the jar. (A small paper or cloth bag will do just as well if the jars are too difficult to procure.)

Think of experiences your students are likely to have in common:

- A story about a game you like to play.
- An adventure on rollerblades, a skateboard, or a bicycle.
- Your first memory.

- Encounters with "bad animals," such as a bee, dog, or cat.
- A scar you have.

Students should pull out a scenario and paste it into their Extreme Writing books. If they run out of things to say about that prompt within the allotted time, they can select another one and continue. However, they should not be allowed to put a prompt back if they pull it out. Remember, immediate fluency is the goal. Students should be able to write something about almost any topic.

Use this Inspiration for only a few days at a time. If you are lucky, this will be another instance that students ask to revisit a writing activity and say, "Aren't we going to do the Extreme Jars anymore?" When that happens, you can mentally pat yourself on the back for once again getting your students to beg for more writing.

Inspiration #3: Be a Character

Project pictures of five characters from Peanuts: Pigpen, Snoopy, Schroeder, Lucy, and Charlie Brown. If students are unfamiliar with these characters, quickly explain who they are and point out that one of the reasons Peanuts has been so popular for so long is because everyone can identify a piece of themselves in one of the characters. Even though all of the characters are nice, they each have a defining characteristic: Pigpen is messy, Snoopy is clever and creative, Schroeder is passionate about his hobby, Lucy is intelligent and organized, and Charlie Brown is trusting and hard working.

Begin with an oral language activity. In groups of three or four, have students choose a character and then think of a time when they acted like that character. Model the process aloud, for example: "I'm a little like Pigpen because, even though my room is very clean, my desk is a total mess." Encourage students to share their stories with one another. Provide about 3–5 minutes for this activity in total.

And the Extreme Writing? Give students a strip of paper with small pictures of each character, and ask them to cut out the character with whom they identified. They should glue the picture in their Extreme Writing books and write an expanded version of how they are like that character. If they run out of steam, they can choose another character and continue writing until they reach the required number of words.

You can use lots of different characters with this Inspiration (e.g., Disney and Pixar characters work very well). Just remember to choose five that are different from one another. Think of qualities people may have, and assign them to the characters by printing key words or phrases underneath.

Inspiration #4: Connect to the Date

Select 10 important dates for the coming year. You can find interesting dates by simply searching online for important dates, events, and anniversaries. Then, when the appropriate dates comes around, the Extreme Writing Inspiration will begin with that story.

For example, on December 17, 1903, the Wright Brothers succeeded in making the first controlled and sustained heavier-than-air flight—120 feet in total. With this as background, show video of this achievement (easily found on YouTube) on December 17, or as close to it as possible. The Extreme Writing prompts might include the following:

- Trips you have taken, both small and large.
- Amazing inventions and changes during your own lifetime and the impact they have had on you.
- Only 66 years passed from the first flight to the moon landing. Write everything you know about things that fly.

There is a great resource called *Writing Down the Days: 365 Creative Journaling Ideas for Young People* that provides writing ideas connected to interesting events that happened on each day of the year (Dahlstrom, 2000).

Inspiration #5: Map of Your Yard

Begin by showing a map of your own yard when you were a child. Put numbers on the map to show locations about which you can tell an interesting story. Tell students where you were raised and explain how to "read" the map. Then tell a story, especially one that might involve events that are outside of your students' experience.

Ask students to draw maps of their own yards in their Extreme Writing books. If they have moved a lot or don't have a yard, provide an alternative approach, such as drawing a map of a memorable play area, park, or playground. Remind students to number at least 5–10 locations on the map. Have students tell a story about one of these locations to a partner, and then have partners switch roles. Allow two minutes for each student to tell his or her story, so four minutes total for this oral activity. The time pressure matters because you don't want students to use up their energy and excitement and then not want to write about it.

Finally, have students write their stories in their Extreme Writing books. Encourage them to include a lot of sensory and supporting details. A week or so later, have them refer back to their maps and write about a different location. They can also create other maps—such as the inside of their house, the neighborhood where they play, or the school and schoolyard—in order to tell more stories.

Inspiration #6: The Excuse

This Inspiration should only be used once, but it is a lot of fun as students tend to enjoy iconoclastic humor of accidenally getting something done while explaining they couldn't do it. There are two ways to start. One is to start with the illustrated book *I Didn't Do My Homework Because . . .*, which contains a different elaborate excuse on each page (Cali & Chaud, 2014). You could also consider giving each student a reduced version of one page and asking them to write an expanded excuse to accompany the illustration. This could morph into an excellent full-scale writing lesson that results in a published class book of crazy excuses.

The other possibility is to use the following poem I wrote as the Inspiration:

It's Really Not My Fault

Well, teacher, now's the time
That I'm telling you in rhyme
My computer did the crime . . .
And my homework isn't done.

I wrote it in my free time
I knew it when I heard the "chime"
My computer did the crime . . .
And my homework isn't done

A power failure big time
A worm or virus (what slime)
My computer did the crime . . .
And my homework isn't done

It's really not my fault.

For this Inspiration, there are not three prompts; instead, there are two required lines. The first line of this piece of Extreme Writing should be "I didn't get my Extreme Writing done because . . ." After that, students should write 200 words (or whatever is required) giving excuse after excuse for why it isn't done. For example: "I was halfway through when my mom called me for dinner, and when I got back I couldn't find it. I looked all over the house and finally found it in the kitchen garbage. I guess I took it down with me, and my dad threw it out. So I started again but when I was playing with my hamster, he made a little 'accident' on the page, so I had to start again. Then my pencil broke and all my pens were out of ink, so I had to . . ." I think you get the idea.

When the required number of words has been reached, students must end with "So that's why I couldn't do it, but— oops—I got it done anyway."

Inspiration #7: Lists

Lists are a great way to grab student interest. Obviously, students will need to elaborate on items they include on their lists, but a list by itself can be a wonderful place to start and an effective Inspiration. Some possibilities include the following:

- Things you are grateful for.
- Things you can do and are good at.
- Your favorite TV shows.
- Things you want to do in your life (i.e., a junior bucket list).
- Movies you love or hate.
- Things you love to do in your free time.
- Foods you love or hate.

An ABC list of attributes that students have or would like to develop could also be absorbing. For example, *A* is for *anger*, *B* is for *bravery*, and so on. Students then add details of what that word might "look like" in their lives right now and in the future. For example:

A is for *angry*. One thing that makes me angry is seeing someone being picked on. The other day on the bus, I noticed some students repeatedly poking the student in front of them and then looking around innocently when he turned around. Someday I might like to be a lawyer who defends the underdog.

Inspiration #8: The Junk Drawer

It's best if this Inspiration is only used once. The surprise of you bringing your own junk drawer is likely to wear out if you do it again, and the reason Extreme Writing Inspirations "work" is their novelty. Bring a "junk drawer" from home to class and talk about what is in it. Explain that almost every home has one. In class, students can write about some of the items in your drawer or imagine they are rummaging through a similar drawer at home.

Three prompts might include the following:

- Describe as many items as you can, including what they are used for and how they might have gotten in the junk drawer.
- You are an archeologist from the future. This junk drawer is all you have; everything else from our civilization has been destroyed. What conclusions might you draw about the civilization that left this final artifact?
- Write a journal entry written by one of the items from the drawer. What did it do in a previous life, how did it

get in the drawer, and how does it feel about the other items in the drawer?

If students have access to a camera and printer, suggest that they include a picture of their particular drawers.

Inspiration #9: Quilting

Provide a version of the following as background for students:

Storytelling goes back to the beginning of spoken language both as a form of entertainment and as a way of keeping the history of a people. When people first settled into cities after the agricultural revolution, there was—for the first time in history—a surplus of food. Specialized jobs arose because people could afford to buy and sell services. One of the jobs that developed was the itinerant storyteller, traveling from town to town and telling stories for money. Think of them as the Spielberg and Lucas of their day.

In India, the storyteller would come into town carrying a quilt that would then be spread out in the center of the village. Each square of the quilt was the prompt for a story. The townspeople would point to a square as a way to request a particular story. In other words, quilting was a method to keep stories alive and share them with as many people as possible.

With this background, have students draw a large hashtag / tic-tac-toe board on a sheet of paper. This will be the basic design of a "quilt" that has room for nine possible stories. Provide students (orally) with about 13 prompts, and have them draw or write their immediate thoughts about one prompt in each square. It should be just enough to remind them of the story after you've presented all of the prompts.

There are two advantages to this strategy. First, every student should have something to write. Second, the quilt can be folded up and put into their Extreme Writing books for future inspiration.

Here are 13 prompts with which you can start your own list:

- A time when you were treated unfairly.
- Schoolyard or summer adventures.
- A story about moving.
- A story of the birth of your brother or sister.
- A time when the weather affected you and your family (e.g., a storm, power outage, fallen tree, flooded basement).
- Encounters with wild animals.
- An experience with a pet.
- A story about a club or team you belong to.
- A time you got into trouble.
- A story about riding a bicycle.
- Something you worked really hard to learn to do.
- Visiting the dentist or doctor.

- An adventure about a time you got lost or when you lost something.

The Internet is replete with thousands of possible prompts. Generally, it is best to think of the environment in which your students live and the experiences they are likely to have had and then use these as a source for engaging prompts.

Another idea is to ask each student to think of three prompts he or she would like to write about. Collect all of these prompts, and create a "master list" to put onto a quilt or into an Extreme Writing Jar.

Inspiration #10: Sayings

Inspirational sayings or aphorisms can also be a good source of Extreme Writing Inspirations. Explain that an aphorism is a short, memorable statement that contains wisdom in a surprising or even amusing form. Then introduce an aphorism, and create or display an image illustrating the aphorism.

One example might be "an apple a day keeps the doctor away." Ask students to work in small groups for two minutes and discuss what they think this saying means and come up with at least two relevant examples. Have groups convene and discuss briefly as a class; this will allow students to link others' ideas to their own experiences and give them more to write about. Finally, present the three prompts:

- Write about a time (or times) when you were sick.
- Write everything you know about foods that help you stay healthy.

- Write about foods you really like and those you don't, including details of why.

Inspiration #11: Artful Writing

For this Inspiration, identify and use famous pieces of art, such as Munch's *The Scream*, Magritte's *Time Transfixed*, Homer's *Snap the Whip*, and Gainsborough's *The Blue Boy*.

For *The Scream*, point out that Munch said he painted the blood-red sunset in the background to represent an infinite scream passing through nature (Aspden, 2012). Possible writing prompts might include the following:

- Write about things that make you scream (e.g., watching scary movies, being tapped on the shoulder unexpectedly, being frustrated, cheering in an audience).
- Write about times when you have been afraid.
- What thoughts do you have about Munch's infinite scream passing through nature? What is there about nature that might be "screaming"?

See my Pinterest page for a collection of 20 pieces of art, complete with prompts (www.pinterest.com/diana32).

Inspiration #12: Picture Book Prompts

Almost any picture book you use with grades 4–9 (e.g., as a model for students to imitate, as a start for rapid research, or for oral language development) can also be the basis of three writing prompts. One example—perhaps used as part of a unit on the history of flight—might be

The Fabulous Flying Machines of Alberto Santos-Dumont (Griffith & Montanari, 2011). After reading this book aloud and discussing why most people remember the Wright brothers but not Santos-Dumont, introduce the following prompts:

- Santos-Dumont was an early aviator. Tell a story about all the forms of transportation you have used.
- Santos-Dumont made public appearances in various parks. Tell a story about a public event or festival you attended.
- The story starts with Santos-Dumont using his dirigible to go shopping for a hat. Tell a story about any chores you do—for yourself or others.

Inspiration #13: Great Advice

Consider asking students to write the ABCs of good advice, which is actually a list of 26 very short prompts. Then, for each piece of advice, students should give a story about themselves or someone else following (or not following) this advice.

- **A**lways be alert.
- **B**e brave.
- **C**are about others.

Alternatively, select a key concept (such as good manners), and provide students with several relevant and appropriate quotes. Ask them to write opinions and stories based on those quotes. For example, you might present the following:

- "Being on time is a matter of good manners."—Ann Landers
- "The hardest job for kids is learning good manners without seeing any."—Fred Astaire
- "Good manners costs nothing and buys everything." —Lady Mary Montague

Ask students to consider and discuss these quotes in small groups. They should then respond to one of them, thinking about what defines good and bad manners today— in elevators, on cell phones, on buses, in cars, in a line, and so on.

What Other Sources of Inspiration Are There?

Almost anything that interests your students can become an Inspiration. Here are some additional possibilities that occurred to me but which I haven't elaborated on in any detail. They may kickstart your own thinking of new Inspirations for your students.

News Stories: Provocative news stories are a great resource. Think of the 6-year-old charged with sexual harassment for kissing a girl's hand or the chicken farmer who paid for DNA testing to prove which neighbor's dog was attacking his chickens. Keep your ears open for interesting and appropriate stories. There are plenty; all you need to do is think of three prompts for the story you choose.

Confucius Says: In China, there has been a recent resurgence of Confucianism—the world's only religion without a deity. This is a chance to enrich the cultural literacy of your students with sayings from the 4th century, such as the following attributed to Confucius: "Learning wthout thought is labor lost; thought without learning is perilous." After students discuss what this means, they could be given prompts such as the following:

- Things you made an effort to learn.
- Things you worry about.
- Ideas you have had that you later found out were untrue.

Benjamin Franklin's 13 Virtues: Ben Franklin, in desiring to improve himself, identified 13 virtues to live by (including temperance, silence, order, and resolution) and then actually tracked his success in achieving them. Extreme Writing has to be partly frivolous, and even though these virtues might skew toward being too "heavy," students can still draw inspiration from them if presented appropriately.

Name That Game: Ask students to write a tutorial for a game they like to play. Tell them not to name the game outright. Have them exchange papers in groups of three, and then challenge classmates to "name that game."

Cartoons: Select funny examples (political cartoons and comic strips both work well) that lend themselves to three prompts and deeper thinking. The possibilities are endless.

Pick a Word: Have students open a dictionary and point to any noun or verb they already know. They should then use synonyms and antonyms for that word as prompts, or simply use that word if it is sufficiently inspiring. Imagine the word they point to is *palette*. They could write about

- Any art experiences you have had.
- Any time you were mixed up (a palette is where you mix colors).
- The most beautiful things you have ever seen.

Where I'm From: Display the sentence starter *I am from...* and 8–10 descriptive words or phrases on the board. Students should use these prompts as clues to write a single vivid detail for each category.

- A detail from your home: I am from yellow kitchen chairs and long curly cord phones.
- A detail from your city: I am from walking train tracks to the stores.
- A detail from your specific location: I am from 1/3 acre of rich black Richmond soil.
- A detail from your yard: I am from harvesting our own potatoes, peas, and corn.
- A detail from money: I am from picking blueberries at 99 cents per pound and eating them all on the way home.
- A detail from food: I am from raiding the refrigerator at night.
- A detail from transportation: I am from biking free across a flat island.

For each line in their "poem" about themselves, students can elaborate with a story that forms their Extreme Writing assignment.

Statistics: Look for an interesting statistic around which you can build three prompts. An example might be: 96% of people making a peanut butter and jelly sandwich spread the peanut butter on first.

- Write about the "logic" of your food. What do you eat first? Last? Do you prepare things in a certain way?
- Write about lunches and dinners. What are your favorite and least favorite foods?
- Write about food diversity in your life. Many Americans now eat foods from many different cultures, such as Mexican, Cuban, Japanese, Chinese, Vietnamese, Thai, German, French, and Italian. Which of these do you eat? Which dishes do you like? Which do you not like?

YouTube: YouTube videos can be a wonderful resource for Extreme Writing. Identify a few short, punchy (and appropriate) videos around which you can develop three prompts that draw from your students' experience.

How Do I Signal It's Time for Extreme Writing?

Make the process fun for you, and it will also be fun for them. Energy is contagious. That's the goal, after all—something so rewarding that students ask for more—and that unobtrusively builds their fluency (i.e., the third leg of the writing process).

Why not create a routine that signals the start of Extreme Writing in an engaging way? Use whatever routine you know will capture your students' interest and make them say, "Oh good, Extreme Writing time!" Here's one way I have used to keep a demanding process fun.

It's a parody to the tune of "All That Jazz" from the musical *Chicago*. Play the original song for students (maybe twice so they are familiar with the music) and then present the alternative lyrics that follow. Explain that you want students to sing these new words loudly over the recording and that you have a very low standard for excellence; volume is most important. This usually makes students laugh and loosens them up to try.

Then have students sing the song for three days in a row just before Extreme Writing. They don't need to sing the whole song—just the first few measures (which follow). Once students are familiar with the song, tune, and lyrics, they should get a surge of anticipatory adrenaline when you play it in advance of Extreme Writing. This increases the feeling that Extreme Writing is a "fun part" of the year that should be anticipated joyfully, which in turn helps create and foster fluency.

Come on cats
And take your notebooks out
And all that jazz

Unless we write them down
Our thoughts go up the spout
And all that jazz

Start to write
This is the perfect spot
Where our notes are cool
And our thoughts are hot
We need a quiet space
This is the perfect place
And all that jazz

Move your pen
And get your brain in gear
And all that jazz
When you clearly think
You never know no fear
And all that jazz

Hold on cats

We're going to make a draft

Every time we write

We're going to hone our craft

We'll make a daily start

And always write with heart

And all that jazz

To give your feedback on this publication and
be entered into a drawing for a free ASCD
Arias e-book, please visit
www.ascd.org/ariasfeedback

ENCORE

FREQUENTLY ASKED QUESTIONS

These questions are the ones I encounter most frequently in my work with teachers.

Can students use the computer for Extreme Writing?

Well, it might be a certain old-fashioned inclination, but I value writing by hand. It could be that the computer makes it too easy to erase, so you start to second guess yourself. It could be that when writing by hand, students can actively see the amount of work they need to do on basic spelling (without the little spell-check miracle). Or it could be that writing by hand is what many famous authors do because they feel it deepens their thinking. Truman Capote, Susan Sontag, John le Carré, Quentin Tarantino, and George R. R. Martin all write in longhand, claiming it forces concentration.

However, most of my reluctance is borne out of the fear of "cut and paste." There's a great cartoon where a student sitting at a keyboard types "Repeat yesterday. Replace hamburgers with Sloppy Joes." If you know how to prevent this, then go for it! I am not a Luddite; in fact, I am quite the opposite. I'm a huge fan of technology, but I'm also a cautious teacher who really wants students to become terrific writers.

If you choose to have students use computers for Extreme Writing, you'll need to establish a different number of target words that aligns with students' typing skills.

Why 20 minutes? Why not 10 minutes or a half hour?

An important thing to develop in writing is what experienced writers call "flow" or being "in the zone." This is when the ideas are just rolling off your pen. The experience should be challenging but only slightly stretch your skills. You need time for flow to develop, and 20 minutes seems to be about right. However, your younger students may not be able to stay focused for that long. During your first few Extreme Writing sessions, observe your students and you should be able to see when they become distracted. You can then adjust the time accordingly. A characteristic of flow is a lack of awareness of one's surroundings that stems from full concentration on the task at hand.

How do I know if Extreme Writing is building fluency?

Use the Rapid Writes as an assessment tool. Students who start the year able to write 100 words may be able to produce 150 words by winter break. Because you want them to write for 20 minutes, this is your opportunity to increase the number of words expected. Students might groan a bit, but they will still be thrilled with themselves. Repeat and reassess at spring break.

Of course, students will naturally improve throughout the year, so perhaps they would have increased speed without dedicated Extreme Writing sessions. Therefore, see if you can persuade a colleague (who is not doing Extreme Writing) to do Rapid Writes at the same times as you. Compare how much faster the "control class" is to see if your Extreme Writing program is having the desired effect: fluency.

How many words can an adult write?

Students may be interested to know how many words an adult can easily write in 20 minutes. You could mention that the typical teacher can write (by hand) about 30 words per minute, which translates to approximately 600 words in 20 minutes. I have teachers in workshops do the Rapid Write and then show how to find the "middle" number, and 28–32 is pretty well it, every time. If your students are old enough, you could suggest that that if they improve enough, they can race you. This usually goes over remarkably well.

Of course, your students have an assigned number of words to write, but they may be interested in the productivity of other writers.

- In his book *On Writing*, Stephen King recommends writing 1,000 words per day, although he himself writes 2,000. "Only in dire circumstances do I allow myself to shut down before I get my 2,000 words" (King, 2010, p. 142).
- In *The Artist's Way*, Julia Cameron (2002) recommends writing three pages every morning before you start your day.
- Erle Stanley Gardner, the author of the Perry Mason series of books, wrote 13 pages a day (Thayer, 2009).

- John Grisham wrote *The Pelican Brief* (about 80,000 words) in 100 days (Thayer, 2009).
- Jack London's daily goal was 1,000–1,500 words (Thayer, 2009).
- Graham Greene wrote exactly 500 words per day. He would even stop mid-sentence when he reached his goal (Thayer, 2009).

What about identified special needs students or English language learners?

For identified English language learners (ELLs) and special needs students, conduct a one-on-one assessment of their writing speed using a Rapid Write. They will participate with others in the class but with their own unique goal number that you know will take them 20 minutes to do. Students using specialized equipment will have a number reflecting what they can do with that machine.

An alternative strategy might be to ask students to increase their goal by one word each day. If necessary, provide students with a scaffolded approach, such as a cloze paragraph or more detailed prompts and sentence starters. Very early ELLs tend to "translate" using the syntax of their primary language. Over-practicing the translation approach through Extreme Writing could inhibit their development of fluent idiomatic English. I recommend reading Judie Haynes's book *Getting Started with English Language Learners* (2007), which contains many practical suggestions for this group and is designed for mainstream classroom teachers rather than specialized ELL teachers.

Are there examples of famous journals I can tell my students about?

Admittedly, there are no famous examples of Extreme Writing. However, there are famous writers of diaries and journals that might inspire students. Every time you are in a cycle of Extreme Writing, you could introduce one of them. "You too may become famous someday, and your Extreme Writing will be really valuable. At the very least, you will be thrilled at how you thought and what you thought about when you are 40."

Here then are nine famous journal writers. Search online for more details about their respective journals you can share with students.

- Anne Frank: Among all diaries, this diary of a Jewish teen in hiding during the Holocaust is probably the most widely read of all diaries.
- Leonardo da Vinci: da Vinci's journals might have a few pages of anatomical drawings, then some research into water flow, an idea for a helicopter, a few sketches for a painting, and so on. Bill Gates bought one of his original journals, *The Codex Leicester*, for 1.5 million.
- Vincent van Gogh: He left his seven journals with his brother/executor, who cut them up and sold them.

- Marco Polo: His writings, which recounted his travels and adventures through Asia, were considered so amazing that they were treated as fiction.
- Joseph Goebbels: Hitler's propaganda minister wrote over 29 volumes, which were stored in the Reichsbank and survived World War II.
- Samuel Pepys: He kept a daily diary for a decade during the 17th century, which has become an important primary source for the era.
- Emily Carr: Her "lost" diary from a 1907 Alaska trip was rediscovered in 2013.
- Beatrix Potter: She started to keep a journal at 15 in a secret code she invented. That code was not cracked until 15 years after her death.
- Buckminster Fuller: This Canadian inventor kept a scrapbook and journal from 1920–1983. It is said he has the most documented life in history.

References

Aspden, P. (2012, April 21). So, what does 'The Scream' mean? *Financial Times*. Retrieved from www.ft.com

Calli, D., & Chaud, B. (2014). *I didn't do my homework because...* San Francisco: Chronicle Books.

Cameron, J. (2002). *The artist's way*. New York: Penguin.

Common Core State Standards Initiative [CCSSI]. (2010). *Common Core State Standards for English language arts & literacy in history/social studies, science, and technical subjects*. Washington, DC: National Governors Association & Council of Chief State School Officers.

Dahlstrom, M. M. (2000). *Writing down the days: 365 creative journal ideas for young people*. Minneapolis, MN: Free Spirit.

Dean, C. B., Hubbell, E. R., Pitler, H., & Stone, B. (2012). *Classroom instruction that works: Research-based strategies for increasing student achievement, 2nd Ed.* Alexandria, VA: ASCD.

Gladwell, M. (2011). *Outliers: The story of success*. New York: Penguin.

Griffith, V., & Montanari, E. (2011). *The fabulous flying machines of Alberto Santos-Dumont*. New York: Abrams.

Haynes, J. (2007). *Getting started with English language learners: How educators can meet the challenge*. Alexandria, VA: ASCD.

King, S. (2010). *On writing: A memoir of the craft*. New York: Simon & Schuster.

Salahu-Din, D. (2008). *The nation's report card: Writing 2007*. Washington, DC: U.S. Department of Education.

Thayer, J. (2009). How many words a day? Retrieved from www.authormagazine.org/articles/thayer_james_2009_04_09.htm

Related Resources

At the time of publication, the following ASCD resources were available (ASCD stock numbers appear in parentheses). For up-to-date information about ASCD resources, go to www.ascd.org. You can search the complete archives of *Educational Leadership* at http://www.ascd.org/el.

The 5-Minute Teacher: How do I maximize time for learning in my classroom? by Mark Barnes (#SF113072)

Encouragement in the Classroom: How do I help students stay positive and focused? by Joan Young (#SF114049)

Essential Ingredients: Recipes for Teaching Writing by Sandra Worsham (#101241)

Real Engagement: How do I help my students become motivated, confidence, and self-directed learners? by Allison Zmuda & Robyn R. Jackson (#SF115056)

Teaching Writing in the Content Areas by Vicki Urquhart and Monette McIver (#105036)

Time to Teach: How do I get organized and work smarter? by Jenny L. Edwards (#SF114067)

Using Writing to Learn Across the Content Areas: An ASCD Action Tool by Sue Beers and Lou Howell (#705175)

Vocab Rehab: How do I teach vocabulary effectively with limited time? by Marilee Sprenger (#SF114047)

For more information: send e-mail to member@ascd.org; call 1-800-933-2723 or 703-578-9600, press 2; send a fax to 703-575-5400; or write to Information Services, ASCD, 1703 N. Beauregard St., Alexandria, VA 22311-1714 USA.

About the Author

Diana Cruchley is an award-winning educator and author who has taught at both elementary and secondary levels. She is a former president of Langley College and the district administrator for professional and community services in Langley District. Among her national awards are the AMTEC (Association for Media and Technology in Education in Canada) and the Canada Post Flight for Freedom Literacy award. Her most recent book, *Shhh! Canadian Scientists and Inventors Rule,* is her first picture book. Diana's practical workshops across western Canada and in the United States are always enthusiastically received. Contact her at dcruchley@gmail.com.

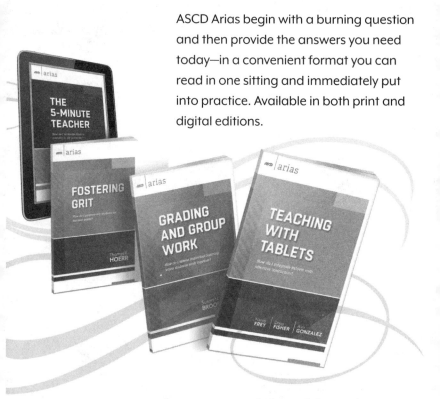